dreaming in color

A Kids Guide to Becoming an Artist

sarah michaels

Copyright © 2023 by Sarah Michaels

All rights reserved.

No part of this book may be reproduced in any form or by any electronic or mechanical means, including information storage and retrieval systems, without written permission from the author, except for the use of brief quotations in a book review.

contents

1. WHAT IS ART AND ILLUSTRATION? ... 5
   Introduction to art and illustration ... 5
   Different forms of art and illustration ... 8
   Brief history of art and famous artists and illustrators ... 11

2. WHY ART MATTERS ... 15
   The role of art in culture and personal expression ... 15
   Stories of how art has influenced the world ... 18
   The therapeutic and emotional benefits of creating art ... 21

3. LEARNING THE BASICS ... 25
   Fundamental art concepts ... 25
   Introduction to different mediums ... 27
   Simple projects and exercises to practice basic skills ... 31

4. DEVELOPING YOUR STYLE ... 35
   Finding and nurturing your unique artistic voice ... 38
   Exercises to experiment with different styles ... 41

5. MASTERING TECHNIQUES ... 45
   Advanced techniques in various mediums ... 45
   Step-by-step guides for complex projects ... 48

6. INSPIRATION AND CREATIVITY — 51
How to find and nurture inspiration — 51
Keeping a sketchbook or idea journal — 54
Creative challenges and prompts — 57

7. FROM HOBBY TO CAREER — 61
Different career paths for artists and illustrators — 61
Introduction to the business side of art — 64

8. ART IN THE DIGITAL WORLD — 69
Introduction to digital art and tools — 69
Basics of graphic design and digital illustration — 72
Online resources and communities for young artists — 75

9. SHARING YOUR ART — 79
Tips for presenting and sharing art in galleries and online — 79
Building an art portfolio — 82
Navigating feedback and criticism — 85

10. INTERACTIVE ART PROJECTS — 89
Step-by-step art projects for various skill levels — 89
Group projects and collaborative ideas — 92
DIY art crafts and activities — 96

Conclusion — 101
Appendex — 111

1 / what is art and illustration?

introduction to art and illustration

HAVE you ever watched a kite dance across an open sky? That's the feeling you get when you experience art in its myriad forms. From the soft swishing sound a paintbrush makes as it dances across a canvas to the steady rhythm of a pencil moving across paper, the world of art has a language where every medium is a unique dialect. Each has its own unique story to tell and together, they celebrate the wonder that is art.

In this chapter, we'll journey across three fantastic lands: Painting, Sketching, and Digital Art. Each of these worlds is magical in its own right, and the best part is, you don't need a ticket to explore them. All you need is a curious mind, an open heart, and the courage to let your creativity soar.

The first stop on our art adventure is the enchanting world of painting. Imagine dipping your brush into a riot of colors, with the blues of the ocean, the greens of the forest, and the yellows of the sun caressing your canvas. Painting is a medium that offers an incredible level of freedom. Whether you are using watercolors, oil paints, or acrylics, each stroke unravels a new masterpiece. Painting is very much like baking a cake - each layer you add gives your creation more depth and flavor. Remember, it's your world; you can paint it however you wish!

Next on our journey is the tranquil realm of sketching. Have any of you looked at a sketch artist and admired the grace with which their pencil sways, creating lovely, intricate designs that bring an image to life? Sketching requires observation, patience, and a knack for capturing details. Whether it be the sharp edges of a geometric shape, the soft curves of a petal, or the intricate lines on a face, sketching can encapsulate every bit of it. If painting is like baking a cake, then sketching is more like making a delicate piece of origami. Both can be beautiful and detailed, but in different ways.

Our final destination is the vibrant and technologically wondrous world of digital art. This is where tradition meets modernity. Digital art is like climbing a rainbow, with a plethora of tools and techniques available at your fingertips. With graphic tablets and stylus pens, you can create stunning, professional works of art without the hassle of cleaning up shards of crayons or spilling paint. Think of it as painting or drawing on a futuristic canvas where you can undo and redo your actions, experiment without wasting resources, and even save your work in an instant! Doesn't that sound like something from a science-fiction novel?

Regardless of the medium you choose, remember this: art is not about perfection; it's about expression. Whether it's painting, sketching, or digital art, each form has its own rhythm, its own pulse, its own reason for being. And no matter which you prefer, what truly matters is that you remain faithful to your own voice, your own style.

different forms of art and illustration

There's a whole world of art and illustration out there rich with different forms, styles, and methods ready for you to explore and master. This chapter delves into this exciting world, explaining various forms of art and illustration, allowing you to find the one that calls out to your own imagination and creativity.

The traditional style takes the lead as the oldest and one of the most respected forms. Traditional art refers to work done using physical materials like paint, brushes, pencils, charcoal, pastels, and pens. It incorporates many styles including realism, surrealism, and abstract, among others. Artists who work in traditional formats create something tangible, something you can touch and feel. This method of creating art has a charm of its own, don't you think?

. . .

However, while traditional art has been around for millennia, the digital method is relatively new but no less exciting or fascinating. In the digital format, instead of physical tools, artists use software and digital devices like tablets and computers to bring their ideas to life. Do the works of art created in this way feel any less? Not at all! The vibrant colors, the exciting shapes, and the life that a digital piece can bring are just as real and impressive.

Digital art incorporates many styles too! There's pixel art, where the artist creates the image pixel by pixel. Doesn't that sound like a lot of fun? There's also vector art, where the artist uses clean, precise lines to illustrate. And let's not forget the enchanting realms of 3D modeling and CGI, where the artists create three-dimensional visuals that feel almost real.

Art and illustration don't stop at these two forms. There are several other types, all fascinating in their unique ways. There's mixed media, where artists combine both traditional and digital elements to craft amazing creations. Add multimedia into the mix, and you get more thrilling opportunities with the incorporation of audio and video into the art piece.

Then there's collage, where artists assemble different forms, shapes, and colors to create a new whole. Collages can be made digitally or traditionally, and both versions are equally delightful to explore. One of the fun aspects of making collages is hunting for the right elements to be part of your masterpiece.

In the world of art and illustration, there's something for everyone. Whether you enjoy the feel of the pencil moving across the paper while you sketch a sunset, the thrill of capturing a moment in an action-filled comic strip, the excitement of creating a mystical beast on your digital drawing pad, or the joy of making a collage from your favorite cartoon clips—the choice is yours.

As we journey further into the world of art and illustration, you will have the opportunity to learn more about these forms, explore how different artists have used them in their work, and eventually decide which forms resonate most with you.

brief history of art and famous artists and illustrators

Our tale commences with the earliest known forms of art - the cave paintings. Drawn on cavern walls by prehistoric people around 40,000 years ago, some of these masterpieces, in France and Spain for instance, continue to astonish us to this very day! Showcasing animals, people, and a variety of symbols, these sketches were the spark that ignited mankind's artistic expression.

Fast forward to Ancient Egypt, around 3000 BC, where art was purposeful and filled with symbolism. Powerful pharaohs, majestic gods, and tales of life beyond death filled the walls of grand pyramids, all painted or carved with immense precision and vivid colours - an astounding sight indeed!

As centuries flew by, art moved to ancient Greece and Rome, where aesthetics and realistic representation of the human form thrived, setting the trend for Western aesthetics. Artists like Praxiteles and Polykleitos immortalised the human form in marble, while others like Apelles executed paintings that were celebrated for their breathtaking realism.

We'll zoom a few centuries further on our historical rollercoaster now. Welcome to the medieval era - beginning around 500 AD. Here, religious themes dominated. Art was used to illustrate Bible stories for those who could not read. With vibrant stained glass windows and meticulously created illuminated manuscripts, artists like Cimabue and Duccio took center stage.

Sometime there around 1400, something incredible happened - the Renaissance! This period signaled a 'rebirth' of art, culture, and science inspired by the classical era. This was when the world received some of its most iconic artists – Michelangelo with his Sistine Chapel ceiling, Leonardo da Vinci with Mona Lisa and The Last Supper, and Raphael with School of Athens. How could we forget Botticelli's Birth of Venus and Jan Van Eyck's Arnolfini

Portrait? The names and their works from this period are too many to count!

Art took a dramatic turn in the 1800s; first with Romanticism, and then Realism, where the focus shifted to everyday life instead of the usual religious or mythical subjects. Artists like Francisco Goya and Gustave Courbet captured the essence of this period wonderfully.

Following that came the period of Impressionsim and Post-Impressionism! Painters like Claude Monet, Vincent Van Gogh, and Paul Cézanne threw all 'rules' out of the window and focused on capturing 'impressions' of scenes and objects. The famous Monet's Water Lilies series and Van Gogh's Starry Night are great examples of this period.

You must have heard about the Cubists, too. Artists such as Pablo Picasso importantly reshaped art in the early 1900s by representing objects from various angles all at once – a distinctive, abstract take on traditional perspectives.

. . .

But what about illustrators? From the early 1900s, illustrators began to gain recognition for their narrative talents. Norman Rockwell, with his illustrations depicting everyday American life, was one such tremendous illustrator. And more recently, illustrators like Mary GrandPré, famous for the fantastical Harry Potter book covers, and Maurice Sendak, creator of Where The Wild Things Are, have captured our imaginations wonderfully.

Now, imagine art in the tech-age! Today, digital art is flourishing, with artists like Loish and Beeple creating breathtaking pieces on their computers and tablets.

You could very well be the next significant name in this history, the one who adds a new splash of colour to the grand ever-changing canvas of art and illustration. The world is your canvas, my friends, are you ready to paint your masterpiece?

2 /
why art matters

the role of art in culture and personal expression

NEXT, will navigate the mesmerizing sea of art. Not simply 'art' you see in galleries or whizzes off an artist's paintbrush, but the layers beneath. This isn't just about what an artist does; it's about why they do it and how it affects us all. You see, art is a complex and powerful tool—it begins as a personal expression and gradually becomes a vital part of our culture.

Ever stopped to wonder why kindergartners immediately reach for colourful crayons or how teenagers in your school love doodling on their notebooks? That's the first peek into personal expression. Each one of us is a 'mini artist' in our own unique way, often using art to show others a glimpse of our world. We sigh, laugh, frown, or jump in joy, all with the help of a few lines and colours. That's the beauty of art—it lets us reveal who we are without having to say a word!

But art is not just about us as individuals, it's also about us as a collective. You see, as we start to share our 'art stories,' they begin to weave into a larger narrative—the narrative of our culture. Have you ever noticed an unusual squiggle or a brilliant colourful mural around your town? Well, they aren't just mere decorations. Each stroke, each colour, each shape narrates a tale about your town's past, its people and their experiences. Art plays a crucial role in telling the story of a culture; it's the enduring voice of communities, societies, and nations, transcending time and space.

Let's hop onto a magical carpet and travel a bit. Have you heard about the cave paintings in Lascaux, France, or the intricate Rajasthani miniatures in India? Those are not just stunning pieces of art, but important historical markers. They tell us about how our ancestors lived, what they cared for, and how they saw the world. Caves became their canvas, and they used crushed berries or charcoal as their medium. Talk about being creative and resourceful!

Or let's take a flight a bit closer to this era. Ever marveled at the pop art of Andy Warhol or wondered at the abstract paintings of Piet Mondrian? They did not just wake up one day and randomly decide to paint soup cans or colourful grids. Their art was a reflection of the rapidly changing society around them. They used their canvases to comment, to question and to reflect on the reality they were part of.

That's the role art plays. It doesn't exist in a vacuum—it's closely linked to the period and place of its origin. The artist isn't just an individual working in isolation but acts more like a mirror, reflecting the society he or she lives in. As a result, we could understand much about a culture's rituals, values, and philosophies through its art.

Now buckle up, as we fly you back to your own neighborhoods. Recall the vibrant art festivals or local exhibits you've attended? Remember the mind-blowing street graffiti or the striking statues in your public parks? They're more than just pleasant encounters. They shape our shared identity and bring us together. Now wouldn't it be pretty dreary and oh-so-bland if cities and towns didn't have these sparks of creativity?

Let's finish off this ride with you, our future artists and illustrators. What makes YOU pick up that sketchbook? What makes your eyes gleam as you swipe that paintbrush against a blank canvas? It's your unique imagination, your emotions, your experiences, and your views. Art becomes an outlet, a stage for you to perform, charm, and captivate the world with your personal expression!

It's your turn now to step into this wondrous timeline of art, to contribute to the expanding panorama of culture through your artwork. It's your time to make the world sit up and listen to your story. And guess what? We can't wait to see what you create, and neither can the world!

stories of how art has influenced the world

Let's dive into some amazing stories that show just how powerful and influential art can be!

The Ancient Echoes of Art

Long ago, before the internet, television, or even books, people were telling stories through art. Imagine walking into a cave over 30,000 years old and finding walls covered with paintings of animals and handprints – like a Stone Age art gallery! These ancient cave paintings, found in places like Lascaux in France, weren't just for decoration; they were a way for early humans to communicate and record their lives. They tell us stories about what was important to those people, from the animals they hunted to the beliefs they held.

Art That Changed Minds

Fast forward to a time when art became a powerful tool for change. During the Renaissance, a period bursting with creativity in Europe, artists like Leonardo da Vinci and Michelangelo didn't just create beautiful works; they changed the way people thought. Their paintings and sculptures showed the beauty of the human body and the natural world, leading to a new appreciation of science and humanism. This shift in thinking helped spark the Renaissance, a time of great scientific discoveries and explorations.

Art as a Voice for the Voiceless

Art hasn't just been about beauty; it's often been a voice for those who weren't heard. In the 1930s, a Mexican artist named Frida Kahlo used her paintings to express her life experiences and emotions. She had a tough life, with lots of health problems, but she turned her pain into powerful art that spoke about issues like identity, gender, and class in Mexico. Her art wasn't just personal; it was political, and it made people think about the world in new ways.

Sarah Michaels

When Art Speaks Louder Than Words

Sometimes, art can say things that words just can't. This was especially true in the case of Pablo Picasso's famous painting 'Guernica'. Created in response to the bombing of a small Basque town during the Spanish Civil War, this enormous painting shows the horrors of war. With its twisted figures and anguished expressions, 'Guernica' brought global attention to the tragedy and became a symbol of peace and anti-war movements.

Art That Brings Us Together

Art has also been a way to bring people together. The Berlin Wall, a symbol of division during the Cold War, became one of the world's largest canvases for graffiti and murals. When the wall came down in 1989, these artworks became symbols of freedom and unity. Today, they remind us of the power of art to express hope and bring people together.

The Digital Art Revolution

In our modern world, art continues to evolve and influence society. With the rise of digital art and the internet, artists can share their work with the world in ways never imagined before. Digital artists like Kehinde Wiley use technology to create stunning portraits that blend traditional styles with contemporary subjects, challenging our ideas about race, power, and identity.

Your Place in the World of Art

Now, let's think about how you can be part of this amazing world of art. Every time you pick up a pencil, a brush, or a stylus, you're joining a long line of artists who have used their talents to make people think, feel, and see the world differently. Whether you're creating a comic, a painting, or a digital masterpiece, your art has the potential to touch hearts and change minds.

Remember, art isn't just about making something pretty; it's about expressing yourself and connecting with others. As you explore your own artistic path, think about the stories you want to tell and the impact you want to have.

the therapeutic and emotional benefits of creating art

Art is a play of colors, lines, shapes and figures. But, it's much more than that. Creating art isn't just about ending up with a beautiful picture when you're done. It's about the journey you take to get there. It's about every brushstroke, every sketch, every splash. Art is emotion. It's therapy. It's stress relief. And for those of you who dream of pursuing a career in art and illustration, it is also passion!

As artists, you might not realize it, but when you engage with art, whether that's sketching, painting, or illustrating, you're doing a whole lot of good to your mind and heart. Let's get into the wonderful benefits of creating art!

To start with, art is an amazing stress buster. Picture this: you've had a long, tiring day. Everything seems to be getting under your skin, and you can't seem to relax. What do you do? Grab your pencils or paints and start creating. As you draw those lines and shapes, color those spaces, and breathe life into your artwork, you'll start to feel a sense of calm seeping in. That's art at work! It absorbs your attention entirely, pushing away your worries, and lighting up your mood.

Next, art promotes self-expression. Remember the time you drew a monster under your bed because you were feeling scared? Or doodled hearts all over your notebook, when you were feeling particularly happy? That's expressing yourself through art! Your artwork serves as a mirror of your feelings and emotions. And the best part is, there's no judgment or criticism involved. Your monsters don't need to be green and your hearts don't have to be red. You're the boss of your art!

Now, let's talk about confidence. When you create something you're proud of, how does that make you feel? On top of the world, right? That's what making art does. It boosts your self-esteem. Every art piece is a completion of a task, and it's a moment of achievement. Your art tells a story - your story. And there's nothing as rewarding as successfully telling your story through your creations.

Lastly, art also helps in problem-solving. Chip whittling away at a lump of wood till it transforms into a beautiful bird, canvas painters mixing colours until they've made the exact shade they want, even comic book artists sketching and resketching a character until they've got it just right – all these activities train the brain to think outside the box. When you're an artist, you're a thinker, inventor, and problem-solver!

In case you're wondering, yes, the therapeutic and emotional benefits of creating art extend to the world of digital art, too! With illustration software and drawing tablets, you can create amazing digital artwork. You still engage your mind and emotions in the act of creating. You still express your thoughts and stories. And most importantly, you continue to experience the joy and satisfaction that art brings.

Now, ask yourself again, why you love creating art? Hopefully, this chapter would have given you more reasons than you started with.

Creating art and pursuing a career in it is more than just producing beautiful pieces. It's about self-discovery, communication, personal growth, and ultimately, healing – it's a beautiful journey of life in colors and lines.

As an art lover, cherish these therapeutic and emotional benefits that creating art gives. Celebrate the joy it brings and use the relief it provides. Keep creating, keep exploring, and keep growing. There will always be a world inside your imagination waiting to be splattered on a canvas or sketched on a paper. Be fearless in your creations.

3 /
learning the basics

fundamental art concepts

COLOR THEORY IS all about how colors interact with each other and how they influence emotions and thoughts. Does the color red make you think of a fast race car or a ripe apple? That's color theory at work!

There are three primary colors in the world: red, blue, and yellow. Toss them around in different combinations, and you can make any color your heart desires! When primary colors are combined, they create secondary colors: green, orange, and purple. Mix a primary color with a secondary one, and voila! You've got yourself a bunch of lovely tertiary colors. It's like a magical mystery tour of colors!

Now, there is something called the color wheel, which is a circle showing how these colors blend into one another. Besides being extremely fun to spin, it's also a great tool for artists to decide which colors complement or contrast each other.

Picture this: If you're drawing a roaring lion, would you want to use colors that make it blend into the background, or would you want colors that make it leap off the page? With a splash of understanding about color theory, you can make your lion practically roar at people as they walk by!

But colors are just the beginning! Once you're armed with your palette of vibrant shades, the next fundamental concept in art is composition. It's an impressive word that basically means how elements are arranged in a piece. An element can be anything from a tree to a sketched out superhero - the fun lies in deciding where to place them!

As an artist, you're also a visual storyteller. With composition, you get to decide how your story unfolds. Think about an exciting comic strip you might want to make. Where do the characters stand? Where does the action take place? Planning out these parts is what composition is all about.

There are techniques that artists use to make a composition appealing to the human eye. Like the rule of thirds – imagine your paper is divided into

9 equal squares, like a tic-tac-toe board. Placing the most important elements of your drawing on the lines of this imaginary grid can create visual interest and balance!

Art, like cooking a fantastic meal, isn't just about the ingredients. It's also about how they're served up! And that's what composition allows you to do. You might have the most beautiful shades of color at your disposal, but without considering the composition, your art piece can end up looking like a haphazard storm of color!

And just like that, you're already on your way to becoming a color theory and composition whiz! These fundamental concepts are stepping stones into the ravishing world of art and illustration. With knowledge about these tucked away, you'll find your creative ideas turning into tangible pieces with more confidence, and your artistic journey will turn more vibrant and interesting.

introduction to different mediums

Just like a chef uses different ingredients to cook up delicious meals, artists use a variety of mediums to bring their visions to life. Let's dive in and discover what these mediums are and how they can unleash your creative potential!

1. Pencils and Graphite: The Classic Choice

When you think of drawing, pencils are probably the first thing that comes to mind. Pencils, made of graphite, are perfect for sketching and detailed work. They come in different hardness levels, from very hard (H) to very soft (B). The harder the pencil, the lighter the line; the softer the pencil, the darker and bolder the line. With just a simple pencil, you can create everything from a quick doodle to a detailed portrait.

2. Charcoal: For Bold and Dramatic Effects

Charcoal is a favorite among many artists for its rich, dark lines and the dramatic effects it can create. It comes in two types: compressed (which is harder and gives a more defined line) and vine or willow (which is softer and great for smudging and blending). Charcoal is perfect for expressive drawing and quick sketches, but be warned – it can get a bit messy!

3. Pastels: A Symphony of Color

Pastels are like the bridge between drawing and

painting. They come in vibrant colors and are used to create soft, painterly effects. There are two main types of pastels: oil pastels, which are creamy and can be blended smoothly, and chalk pastels, which are drier and perfect for delicate, powdery textures. With pastels, you can create colorful artworks that are full of life.

4. Watercolors: Delicate and Translucent

Watercolor paints are known for their translucent quality and the way they blend fluidly on paper. They can create effects that no other medium can, from subtle washes of color to bright, bold strokes. Watercolors require a bit of practice to control, but once you get the hang of them, they're incredibly rewarding to work with.

5. Acrylic Paints: Versatile and Quick-Drying

Acrylics are a popular choice for artists of all levels. They're water-soluble but become water-resistant when dry, which means you can layer them without worrying about smudging the layers underneath. Acrylics dry quickly, are easy to clean up, and can be used on a variety of surfaces, making them super versatile.

· · ·

6. Oils: The Traditional Painter's Choice

Oil paints have been used by artists for centuries. They take longer to dry than acrylics, which allows for more time to blend and work with the paint. This can be both a challenge and an advantage – it's great for creating smooth, blended effects but requires patience and planning. Oil painting can seem a bit daunting at first, but it's a rewarding medium to explore.

7. Digital Art: The Modern Frontier

In today's world, digital art has become a major medium in its own right. Using a tablet and stylus, artists can create anything they can imagine, from illustrations to animations. Digital art is great because you can experiment endlessly without worrying about wasting materials. Plus, it offers tools and options that traditional mediums can't, like undo buttons and layers.

8. Mixed Media: Mixing It Up

Why stick to one medium when you can mix several? Mixed media art involves combining different materials and techniques in one artwork. You could mix painting with collage, or drawing with digital elements – the possibilities are endless. Mixed media is all about experimentation and finding unique ways to express your ideas.

simple projects and exercises to practice basic skills

Drawing and sketching are just like playing a sport or an instrument; practicing can do wonders. And guess what? It's actually fun! The best thing about art is that there are no wrong answers. A poof of smoke can float like a fluffy cloud, or streak across your paper like a dragon's hot breath; it's all up to your imagination.

First off, let's practice with some basic shapes. Have you ever noticed how everything around us is made up of shapes? The book you're reading, the chair you're sitting on, even the slice of apple you might have eaten for lunch. Grab your sketchbook, pencil, and eraser. Start by drawing simple shapes like circles, squares, triangles, and rectangles. Once you have a good feel for it, challenge yourself to make more complex shapes, like stars or polygons. Remember, it's not about perfection, it's about practicing and developing confidence in your skills.

Our second exercise is to draw an object from your surrounding. Don't jump off for a spacecraft or T-rex just yet; let's go with something simple like a book, a mug, or a pair of glasses. Pay attention to how the shapes you learned to draw come together to create these objects. You see, drawing isn't that complicated! It's all about breaking down complex objects into basic shapes.

For the third exercise, let's play around with shading. Draw an apple or any other simple object with a definite shape and try to add some shadows to it. This will add depth and make it look three-dimensional. Take note of where the light might be coming from and shade accordingly. This simple technique can take your artwork from plain to looking like it's popping out of the page!

Now we're going to kick things up a notch. Draw your favorite cartoon character or a superhero! Remember, you don't have to create an exact replica. Focus more on capturing the essence of the character. It could be the way they stand or the twinkle in their eyes. Don't worry if it doesn't turn out as you've imagined on the first go. That's perfectly okay. Just go for it again, and remember, you're allowed to erase and start again!

Lastly, let's experiment with different mediums. If you have some paints, crayons, or colored pencils lying around, try recreating one of your drawings using these. Notice how each medium results in a different look and feel. There are so many different mediums in art, and you might just discover your favorite one here!

4 /
developing your style

EXPLORING various art styles

Realistic artists, just like detectives, are experts at observation. They'll pick up on the smallest details — the way light bounces off a raindrop or how wrinkles tell a person's age. Artists who love Realism strive to capture the world exactly as it looks. They focus on fine details, accurate colors, and the effects of light and shadow.

From Realism, we move toward the bright, bold, and sometimes unexpected world of Abstract art. What if I told you that in this style, a few scattered lines and colors could represent a dancing peacock or a bustling city? Abstract art doesn't try to look like real life. Instead, it uses shapes, colors, forms, and gestural marks to achieve its effect. It's open to interpretation, and that's what makes it exciting!

Next, we journey into the realm of Expressionism, where artists express their feelings and emotions rather than replicating the world around them. These artists might distort details or exaggerate colors to provoke certain emotions or create a mood. But remember, there are no right or wrong feelings in art.

Now, let's fast-forward a bit in history and meet the Pop Art style. If you love comic books, advertising, and popular culture, then you're going to adore this art style! Pop Art is known for its vibrant colors and often includes images of celebrities, everyday objects, and elements from mass media. Think of it as bringing a slice of everyday life onto the canvas!

Have you ever looked at a landscape or a person and thought of them as a collection of shapes and colors? That's exactly what Cubism, our next art style, presents! Instead of showing objects from one viewpoint, Cubist artists show objects from multiple viewpoints at the same time. Exciting, isn't it?

Continuing our exploration, we land on Surrealism, an art style that could give your dreams and nightmares a visual form. Surrealists let their imagination fly, creating scenes that may seem bizarre or beyond reality. If you love the idea of making dreamy landscapes or impossible creatures, then consider exploring this style further!

Lastly, we'll explore one last style — Minimalism. Here, artists take simplicity very seriously. The aim is to strip everything down to its essential quality and achieve simplicity. Minimalist artists use limited color palettes, simple shapes, and avoid any unnecessary details. It's about less being more.

Phew, we've come a long way, haven't we? Remember, these are just a few of the many art styles existing worldwide. Each of these styles has numerous sub-styles too. The art world is vast and fluid, meaning there's always room for new ideas and styles to bloom.

As an artist, you should never stop exploring and experimenting, just like an adventurer who is forever on a quest. Remember that every art style started with an idea and a brave individual or group of individuals ready to define their interpretation of art. You're an essential part of this grand art adventure. So grab your sketchbooks and paints, and continue to challenge yourselves.

Sarah Michaels

finding and nurturing your unique artistic voice

You know how your voice sounds different from your friends? Well, something similar happens in the world of art. Every artist has their own unique way of sketching, painting, or sculpting. That special touch that distinguishes your art from others is what we call your artistic voice. It's more than just the style, medium, or subject you commonly use. It's your feelings, your ideas, your background, and your personality mirrored into your creations. It's what tells the world, "Hey, look! This piece was created by me!"

Let's get started and find ways to discover that unique artistic whisper of yours. First, let me tell you one important thing: there's no rush. Finding your artistic voice takes time, practice, and a bit of soul-searching. Some people find it quickly, while others take a while. Regardless of how long it takes, it's a journey well worth it.

A great starting point is to observe your favorite artists. There's a reason their work resonates with you. Maybe it's their choice of color; maybe it's their line work. Whatever it is, take some time to study and admire their work. Learn from their techniques and compositions. It's okay to emulate them in the beginning— it's part of learning. But remember, the goal is not to become a copy of another artist, but to understand what draws you to their work and use that knowledge as a stepping stone to find your own voice.

Now, let's take a step deeper. Your artistic voice is an expression of your deepest self. So, don't hesitate to do some introspection. What are your favorite things? What are you passionate about? These can be simple things like your favorite color, pet, or storybook character. Or they can be deeper, like emotions you feel strongly, causes you care about, or dreams that inspire you. Pour these passions and dreams onto your canvas. Express those feelings in your illustrations. This honesty in expressing yourself will leave a powerful imprint on your work.

Experimenting is another way you can discover your artistic voice. Feel free to play around with different styles and techniques. Dabble in realism, and then jump into cartooning. Try out watercolors, and then switch to acrylics. Experiment with digital drawing, if you're interested. Each of these experiences will add a new layer to your artistic identity. As you experiment, you'll discover what feels the most natural, enjoyable, and expressive to you.

That could very well be the key to your unique artistic voice.

Remember, while it's important to find your artistic voice, it's equally important to nurture it. Nurturing your artistic voice means continuing to dive deep into the art world, challenging yourself to learn new techniques, and allowing yourself to grow as an artist.

One way to nurture your artistic voice is to practice regularly. Just like playing a musical instrument or learning a new sport, developing your artistic skills takes time and practice. Set aside time each day to draw or paint. And remember, don't be too harsh on yourself when the results don't match up to your expectations. The idea is to keep exploring and improving.

Another aspect to nurturing your art is receiving and giving constructive feedback. Have those trusted friends or mentors? Share your work with them and be open to their feedback. Their perspectives could bring fresh insights and ideas to your work. But also learn to give feedback to others. This will help you understand the art better and nurture your own voice.

Take care of your imagination like it's a precious garden, water it daily with new experiences, impressions, and ideas. Art is essentially a reflection of life. Watch movies, read books, visit art galleries or even parks. Engage with the world of visual storytelling. These experiences will feed your creativity and help you see the world through an artistic lens.

Last but not least, love your unique voice. Being an artist means you will have to deal with both praise and criticism, and it's vital that you hold your own voice high above all else. So, even if others don't fully understand your work yet, keep creating. Be proud of your unique stamp, your artistic voice.

exercises to experiment with different styles

To help you explore, we've assembled some fun exercises. But remember! These are designed to push you out of your comfort zone. You might not create a masterpiece from the get-go, and that's fine! After all, creativity is about journeying into the unknown and uncovering new territories.

1. Coloring Outside The Lines

Charming imperfections can give your work personality. Let's start with an exercise where you intentionally take your coloring outside of the lines. Draw a simple object like an apple or a tree, and when you add color, dare to dance outside the defined borders. Try this with different art mediums - how does color behave outside the lines in watercolor painting versus colored pencils?

2. Abstract Still Life

Abstraction is all about seeing things differently. For this exercise, arrange some objects to create a still life. But instead of drawing exactly what you see, experiment with exaggerating shapes, bending lines or even rearranging certain parts. Turn your teapot into a skyscraper or transform your apple into a rolling hill. The objective here is to reinterpret reality.

3. Comic Strip Character

Comic strip characters have a simplified yet emphatic style. Choose a favorite character or invent a new one, and draw it in ten different ways. Change shapes, proportions, or even styles of other famous cartoonists. This will help you understand different approaches to character design.

4. Opposite Day

For this little experiment, draw something in a way you normally wouldn't. If you usually use sharp, angular lines to draw, try using only fluid, curved lines, or vice versa. Do you usually leave a lot of whitespace in your illustrations? Try filling the entire page. This exercise helps you experience artmaking from an entirely different perspective.

5. Collage Landscapes

You'll need magazines, scissors, and glue for this one. Cut out colors, textures, and pictures that you like and use them to make a landscape scene. Play with scale and perception. This will help you consider different textures and materials in your work.

Just keep practicing and soon these artistic expressions will become second nature. And don't forget to have fun throughout this adventure. Understand that it is okay to make mistakes, and it is also okay not to love what you create every single time. That is called learning, and it makes you a better illustrator in the long run.

5 / mastering techniques

advanced techniques in various mediums

IF YOU'VE EVER WATCHED a superhero movie, then you know how exciting it can be when the hero discovers they have more than one power. Imagine if Spider-Man suddenly found out he could not only shoot webs but also fly, or if Harry Potter learned he could talk to animals in addition to doing magic! It's just like that with art; once you master one medium, you can explore new ones and unlock even more of your creativity.

In this chapter of our journey, we're going to learn about advanced techniques in different artistic mediums. Buckle up and adjust your creative helmets; this is going to be exciting!

Let's start by painting a picture (pun intended) about oil painting. This is an old-world technique with dateless charm. Oil paints are loved for their vivid colors and the depth they can bring to a painting. But getting them to do what you want takes a little bit of science. This is because oil paints take a while to dry, which means you can go back and change things around, add more details, or even start over if you need to. But be patient, your masterpiece can take days or even weeks to be completely dry!

You'll need special brushes for oil painting, ones with long handles and stiff bristles. Painting with oils is about building layers, starting thin and gradually adding more paint. Picture it like building a LEGO tower; you start with the base and keep adding bricks one at a glance until you have a towering skyscraper. The same thing goes for oil painting.

Next stop on our medium adventure: watercolor painting. It's like the playful cousin of oil painting. Watercolors are transparent and light. This means that the white of the paper shows through your paint, creating a beautiful, luminous look. It's like magic! But like any magic trick, it takes practice. The tricky part is learning how much water to add. Too much, and your colors are too pale. Not enough, and your paint won't spread properly.

Watercolor paintings start light, and then you gradually add darker colors. This is the opposite of oil painting, where you can start dark and lighten as you go. Imagine your watercolor painting like a sunrise, gently becoming brighter and more vibrant as the sun climbs in the sky.

Let's switch gear and talk about a popular medium among young artists: digital art. This is art made with software on computers or tablets. It's like the newest superhero on the block, with flashy tricks and tools. You can undo mistakes, use layers, and even create animations. The versatility of digital art makes it a favorite for many creators around the globe.

One thing to remember with digital art is that it has a different feel compared to traditional art. It's like trading in your bicycle for a skateboard, it gets you to the same place, but the ride is really different. With digital art, you won't have the feel of paint on a brush or the sound a pencil makes on paper, but you'll gain a whole new world of tools and effects to play with.

Finally, let's check out one of the oldest (and possibly most fun) mediums: sculpture! With sculpture, you can create 3-dimensional art that people can walk around, touch, and see from every angle. It's like going from a flat map to a model globe. Suddenly, everything is more real and tactile.

Sculpture is a bit like playing with Play-Doh when you were a toddler, but on a more epic scale. You can use clay, wood, metal, or even ice to create your sculptures. Good sculpture is about looking, imagining, and understanding shapes and forms. It's a dance of fingers and thumbs to shape, scrape, and smooth your material into your masterpiece.

Have you noticed a theme? Each medium requires a different way of thinking, different skills, and different tools. But they all require practice and imagination.

step-by-step guides for complex projects

Step 1: The Grand Plan

Every impressive piece of art begins with a grand plan. This step is all about organizing your thoughts and sketching out your ideas. Don't stress about making a masterpiece straight away; use it as a roadmap. It could be a rough sketch, a bullet-point list of things you want to include or a storyboard; whatever helps to put the chaos of creativity into order.

Step 2: Gather Your Materials

Once your plan is in place, it's time to gather your weapons - I mean, materials. Each project will require a different set of tools, from pencils and markers to paints and brushes. It's also essential to ensure your workstation is clear, clean, and well-lit. Remember, a cluttered desk equals a cluttered mind!

Step 3: Master the Fundamentals

Do you remember the basic elements of art we discussed in previous chapters - lines, forms, shapes, colors, texture? They are your best friends as you march into battle with complex projects. All art, no matter how varied, relies on these key ingredients. Make sure you can use these before you move onto the advanced stuff!

Step 4: Practise Parts of the Whole

This is my secret tip just for you - shhh! When confronted with a complex project, don't attempt it all in one go. Break it down into manageable parts. If it's an intricate landscape, practise drawing trees, mountains, or water bodies separately. Then bring them all together in your masterpiece.

Step 5: Create Your Draft

With enough practice, you can now combine all the parts. Make a full draft of your project. Don't worry about perfection at this stage; this is your chance to adjust the composition, tweak the color scheme, and ensure it all flows together. Take your time.

Step 6: Refine and Detail

Now's the time to put in those finishing touches, the fine details that bring your art to life. This is often the most time-consuming part, but it's also where your project will start to shine. And remember, patience is key – don't rush, let the art of detailing take its course.

Step 7: Seek Feedback

Once you're satisfied with your work, show it to a friend, family member, or art teacher. Don't be shy; every great artist needs input from others. Take their feedback seriously but remember that art is subjective. What others see or say can sometimes give you an entirely different perspective. Use it to improve.

Step 8: Final Touches

The last step is to incorporate any changes based on the feedback, do your final checks, and voila! You've now conquered your complex project.

6 / inspiration and creativity

how to find and nurture inspiration

THINK about your favorite artist or illustrator. Do you ever wonder where they get their ideas? From a secret idea shop in the sky, perhaps? Well, they actually find inspiration from their surroundings, feelings, thoughts, and experiences. And guess what? You can do the same.

There's a popular saying that nothing comes from nothing. That's especially true when we're talking about inspiration. That's why the first step in finding inspiration is exposure—exposure to all sorts of things. Ideas hardly spring from an empty mind! You need to feed your brain a steady diet of different experiences to keep it fit and ready to get its creative juices flowing.

Expose yourself to a whole host of experiences. Visit museums, read books, watch movies, explore nature, engage in sports, listen to music, or try out new recipes - there's no limit to what you can try. The more variety, the better. It's like filling your artist's toolbox with an assortment of colors. The more colors you have, the more vibrant your creations will be.

Creating a mood board can greatly help in nurturing your inspiration. Gather some magazines, cut out images, photographs, headlines, or phrases that catch your eye. Arrange them on a bulletin board, door, or wall, and voila! You have a mood board. Each time you look at it, it could spark a new idea or two, or even remind you of a forgotten one.

It's also useful to create an "inspiration journal". Write down all your thoughts, ideas, dreams, and whatever else comes to mind. Reflect on experiences that make you feel a certain way - happy, sad, excited, dejected - and write them down. Remember to sketch, doodle, or paint in your journal as well. At times, words aren't enough to capture an emotion or an idea, but a quick sketch might do the trick!

Now, let's talk about nurturing inspiration. You may ask, "What does that even mean?" Think of your inspiration like a tiny seed. With the right conditions, this seed can grow into a beautiful, full-grown tree.

Nurturing inspiration requires time and effort, just like tending to a tree does. Start by setting aside some time each day to focus solely on your ideas. This could be first thing in the morning when you wake up, or right before bedtime. Whenever it is, make sure you're free from distractions and can focus on letting your thoughts flow.

Experiment with your ideas, and don't be afraid to make mistakes. There's a little secret I'd like to share: every art piece implies its own possible universe of mistakes just waiting to become unexpected masterpieces. Remember, even the renowned artist Thomas Edison once said, "I haven't failed – I've just found 10,000 ways that don't work."

Most importantly, have patience! The inspiration tree does not grow overnight. There will be times of plenty, when you feel like the ideas just won't stop coming, other times it'll seem like your brain has forgotten how to create entirely. But that's all part of the process, my young artist. During your dry spells, revisit your mood board and inspiration journal, they're friends who'll lend a spark when you need it the most.

Remember to keep your heart and mind open at all times; you never know when and where inspiration will strike. It might come from the flight of birds across the sky, a hidden pattern in the clouds, or a rumble of thunder on a stormy day. The important thing is always to be ready to catch the muse when she comes flitting by.

The secret to finding and nurturing inspiration lies in two simple mantras: explore everything and fear nothing. With these in your artist's repertoire, your creativity will soar. High above the clouds, into the infinite realms of the sky, only then will you find the kind of inspiration that fuels the mightiest of masterpieces.

Finding and nurturing your inspiration is one of the most intimate and enriching journeys you'll undertake in your life. It's an incredible superpower, and with it, you can accomplish great feats, explore unknown territories, and create marvels that will light up the world.

keeping a sketchbook or idea journal

An Idea Journal - is a lot like a secret diary but instead of words, it is full of your unique sketches and cool doodles! Always remember, it can be a piece of a cloud, a weird-shaped rock, or even an unusual tree trunk. Anything your heart would love to draw. It serves as a waiting room for your thoughts that turns into beautifully threaded art. Isn't that exciting?

Now, to the sketchbook - your very own platform for experimenting, making mistakes, and learning, because without a stumble, there's no progress, right? Start creating your masterpiece in your sketchbook, a character, an enchanted scenery perhaps, or how about a self-portrait, warts and all? Anything goes in your sketchbook, it's yours to create and learn from!

Let's switch gears towards the "how-to" part, shall we?

Starting can sometimes seem like the hardest part, the land of the blank page may look daunting but trust me, it's also full of promises. Don't overthink it. Pick up that pencil, marker, crayon or whatever is your favorite, and let your hands do the talking. You don't have to be an expert to fill a sketchbook or an idea journal. Why? Because it's not a performance, it's a practice.

On the pages of your sketchbook, feel free to doodle, draw, color, make comics, write down observations, or even stick interesting things you find like a beautiful feather or a unique leaf!

Remember, each page is a journey and the rule here is - there are no rules!

Coming to the idea journal - use it as a playground for your imagination and creativity. If you see a strange looking cloud, draw it! If you thought of a funny character, bring it to life! Maybe you could sketch out the magical world within your mind. Ideas are everywhere, so keep your eyes and ears wide open, my young observer!

Beneath all this fun, you are actually doing a very important job. You're creating a warehouse of your thoughts and ideas that you can always come back to for inspiration. Greater than any treasure chest, it is a wealth to cherish in your career as an artist or illustrator.

One last piece of advice - carry your sketchbook or idea journal everywhere. You never know when a fantastic idea might strike. It can be at a park, school field trip, or even just lazing around at home!

Remember, when you start filling these pages, you're not just doodling. The sketchbook or idea journal is your doorway to the artist's kingdom. You become a keen observer, an inspired communicator, and a curious explorer. You'll begin to see the world through an artist's eyes—not just looking, but truly seeing.

And if you feel stuck or lost sometimes, that's OK. Just turn over a new page and start afresh. After all, it's not the final picture, but the journey of creating, which is the real art.

Pause your reading here, go grab your sketchpad, or an idea journal and get the ball rolling!

Down the lane, years from now, when you look back at these sketchbooks and idea journals, you'll view them not just as pages filled with doodles and sketches, you will see them as memories, thoughts, and ideas that shaped you, took you places, and maybe even changed the world through your art!

Off you go, keep exploring, keep learning, and don't forget - your art, your rules! Keep sketching!

creative challenges and prompts

Before we move ahead, there's a little secret I want to share. Every artist, even the most skilled and prolific ones, hit a creative block now and then. They may seem to run out of ideas or may find themselves staring at a blank canvas, unsure what to create. It happens to everyone and is completely normal. But don't you worry! That's what prompts and challenges are for. So let's navigate the magical world of art and illustrate most delightfully.

1. Challenge No.1: 'Create Your Superhero':

Children, we all grew up falling in love with superheroes and dreaming of possessing their extraordinary powers, didn't we? Here's your chance! Unleash your super imagination and invent your own superhero. Decide on their powerful abilities and their trademark style. Don't forget about their special attire that makes them stand out from the crowd!

2. Challenge No.2: 'Design an Imaginary City': Ever thought of a magical city or an alien hub? Here's your chance to be a city planner for a day. Design an imaginary city based on your vision. Perhaps it floats in the sky, or maybe it's underwater or is it on a different planet altogether? It's all up to you, so let your creativity flood the canvas!

3. Prompt No.1: 'Draw Your Best Friend As An Animal': This one is going to be fun! Think about your best friend. Now think of their characteristics. Are they cunning like a fox or brave like a lion? Maybe they are slow and steady like a tortoise, or jumpy like a kangaroo! Now sketch your best friend, but as the animal that matches their personality.

4. Challenge No.3: 'Imagine a New Creature': Can you picture a creature that has a horse's head, a kangaroo's body, and a peacock's tail? Or do you want to mix and match different animals to form a

new creature? Go ahead! The world is yet to see this creature through your illustration.

5. Prompt No.2: 'The Time Travel Machine': Construct a time machine that can transport you back to the age of dinosaurs or maybe to the future. How would this machine look? Is it as simple as a wristwatch, or as complex as a space shuttle? Enjoy illustrating your version of the time voyage!

Remember, every prompt or challenge is a starting point. What you create from there is limited only by the boundaries of your imagination. The purpose is to stir your creativity and guide it into a direction. Don't worry about making it perfect, though. Art, after all, is a reflection of how you see the world, and there are no right or wrong ways of seeing things.

One more thing, just a friendly tip from my side: don't rush! Let your ideas marinate. It's not a race; it's a relaxing sail across the creativity sea. Take your time; explore the ideas that these prompts and challenges bring up. Let them simmer in your mind. And when you feel ready, begin with the tip of your pencil on the canvas, and let your creativity do the magic!

The creative journey ahead holds loads of fun-filled experiences. Exciting, isn't it? These creative challenges and prompts are meant to help you create, think out of the box, and most importantly, have fun! Cherish each prompt and each stroke of your pencil. Believe me, breakthroughs happen when we are having fun. When we enjoy the process of creating, the results, too, turn out to be fantastic.

7 /
from hobby to career

different career paths for artists and illustrators

ARE you ready to embark on an exciting journey to explore the different career paths for artists and illustrators? Yes, you heard right. Art isn't just about wearing a smock and splashing paint on a canvas. It's much more than that! Art and illustrations play a vital role in many industries and fields. You'll be surprised to see where your creativity and imagination can guide you.

Our first stop - the wonderful world of animation! Imagine creating characters that seem to come to life on the big movie screen. Isn't it exciting? An animator or a storyboard artist brings life to characters and stories. If you heard of movies like

"Frozen" or "The Incredibles", then you've seen the incredible work of animators and storyboard artists. For those of you with a flair for technology and love creating characters, this might be the dream job you never knew you'd want!

Now, let's cruise through the vibrant streets of advertising. Here, the artists and illustrators are the superheroes. They create eye-catching designs and logos that eventually become the identity of a brand. Whether it's a cereal box or a giant billboard, communicative designs are everywhere, thanks to these artistic geniuses. Companies rely on the creativity of these artists to capture the attention of potential customers. So, if you enjoy creating designs that share a message, hop in! The field of advertising could be the right path for you.

Ever wondered who designs those catchy and cool covers of your favorite books or magazines? A mighty 'thank you' to our graphic artists and illustrators! Their creative genius gives us the much-needed visual treat and entices us to delve into a good read. These artists have an enormous responsibility to deliver the essence of a story through their visual depiction succinctly. So, if you're someone who loves storytelling and creating powerful visuals, this career path could be a great fit.

Let's not forget about the video game industry. From creating unique characters to detailing enchanting landscapes, game designers make the magical realms we lose ourselves in when we play video games. If you're a gaming enthusiast and love creating fantastical worlds, becoming a game designer could be your game-winning move!

Now here's a career path that might get your heart racing - a cartoonist. Cartoonists use their skills to entertain and, sometimes, educate people. Cartoons can end up in your local newspaper, a popular magazine, or even on a website. If you enjoy making others smile with your witty, funny, or insightful sketches, a career as a cartoonist might just be what you're looking for.

How about fashion illustration, you might ask? Fashion illustrators help create and dictate fashion trends used by designers around the world. From sketching initial clothing designs to creating detailed drawings for a fashion magazine, they play a crucial role in the fashion industry. If you love fashion and sketching, this could be your runway to success!

Our final stop is the realm of teaching. Yes, you can use your skill and passion for art to inspire new generations of enthusiastic, young artists. Art teachers help kids discover their creative potential and guide them on their artistic journey. If you love sharing knowledge as much as creating art, becoming an art educator could be your masterpiece.

As you can see, art and illustrations are not confined to any one direction. It's a creative maze where you can explore various paths and avenues, each one as rewarding and exciting as the other. So, don't let the word 'artist' limit your imagination. You can be a game designer, a cartoonist, a graphic artist, or even a teacher! The choice is yours. Determine what excites you the most, align it with your skills, and voila, you'll find a rewarding career that's just right for you.

introduction to the business side of art

Selling art, earning commissions, and understanding the market dynamics can sound overpowering at first. But hey, don't fret! Like mastering any new medium, with a little patience and practice, you'll find navigating the business side of art is just another way to express your creativity.

First, let's demystify the term 'commission.' In the art world, a commission refers to the act of hiring an artist to create a specific piece of artwork.

It is usually well-detailed, with instructions about what the client expects. Commissions can be exciting! Why? They let you explore new territories of creativity while getting paid for it. Think of it as getting a ticket into an art adventure, tailored just for you!

Getting your first commission can be thrilling, but it's essential to communicate clearly with your clients. Understand their ideas, their visions, have them clarified, and make sure you're comfortable with the expected outcome. Keep in mind that revisions are part of the process. Be flexible, yet don't forget to value your work.

How does one obtain commissions, you ask? Well, your personal network is your strongest ally. Friends, family, neighbors, or people who already appreciate your art can be your first set of clients. Social media too provides a vast, easily accessible platform where you can showcase your work and approach potential clients. Remember, every successful artist was once a beginner.

Now let's take a turn and walk down the alley of selling your creations. Art isn't just about making pretty things. It's about creating items of value, and that includes monetary value too. Whether it's selling paintings, prints, or designs for T-shirts, artists can engage in a plethora of ways to turn their creations into a source of income.

To sell your art, you need to find a market for it. Local craft fairs, art festivals, and online marketplaces such as Etsy offer great starting points to showcase your work to the world. Another wonderful platform is a personal website or a blog, which adds an air of professionalism to your profile.

Now, for the bit most budding artists find tricky – pricing. Deciding on a price for your work requires taking into account the time, materials, and expertise involved in its creation. It's crucial not to undersell yourself. Remember, your work reflects your skill, dedication, and creativity; it carries unique value that only you can offer.

Learning about the business side of art also involves comprehending copyright laws. As the creator of your artwork, you own the copyright, which means others cannot reproduce or distribute your work without your permission. Copyrights help secure your art from infringement. So, it's important to recognize and protect your legal rights.

Lastly, let's decipher art licensing. Imagine your vibrant, whimsical artwork on coffee mugs, keychains, stationery, and even shower curtains!

Licensing your art means you're giving a company the right to reproduce your art on their products. In return, you receive a royalty fee. Art licensing can open a whole new universe of opportunities and income streams for artists.

Navigating the business side of art might seem like sailing through uncharted waters. But remember, every journey starts with a simple step. Your passion for art, combined with an understanding of how to create value, can transform your creativity into financial returns.

8 /
art in the digital world

introduction to digital art and tools

WHEN I TALK about digital art, I mean taking pencils, paints, and sketchbooks and transferring them onto a computer screen. Imagine the ability to erase any mistake with a quick click or to duplicate an element of your artwork without needing to draw it all over again. The possibilities are endless, and that's what makes digital art so fascinating!

How Does Digital Art Work?

Let's start with the basics. How does one create art digitally? Instead of traditional art materials, artists use specific tools like a drawing tablet and a stylus pen, which connects to a computer. Then, with the help of certain software (that's a fancy term for computer programs), they translate their creative ideas into digital reality.

They sketch on the drawing tablet just as they would sketch on a physical piece of paper, and the images appear on the screen. Cool, isn't it? And yes, just like a real sketchbook, you can fill up as many 'pages' as you want in this digital sketchbook.

Introduction to Digital Art Tools

Now let's get to know the tools we'll need in our digital art adventure. There are a lot of different tools available out there, but don't worry, you won't need them all. I'm going to introduce you to a few essentials to get you started.

1. Drawing Tablet: Imagine a flatter, slimmer version of your sketchbook, but this one connects to your computer. That's your drawing tablet! This is a touch-sensitive device that captures the motion of your stylus (remember, that's your digital pen), allowing you to draw on its surface which will then appear on your computer screen.

2. Stylus: Think of this as your magic wand. The stylus is like a pen or pencil, only wiser. Its tip is pressure-sensitive allowing you to create thicker or thinner lines depending on how hard you press and that's not something you can easily achieve with an ordinary pencil, isn't that cool?

3. Software: If the drawing tablet is your canvas and the stylus is your brush, then the software is like your colors. And guess what? There are even more options here! Software like Adobe Photoshop or Procreate offer artists a variety of tools to create, edit, and polish their digital artwork.

Try not to feel overwhelmed by the different tools and options. Just as you learned to differentiate between watercolor and acrylic paint, with practice, you'll get the hang of these digital art tools too.

Is Digital Art Better than Traditional Art?

Well, that's like asking if an apple is better than an orange. They're simply different! And you don't have to choose between one or the other. Like many artists, you can enjoy and practice both. The beauty of digital art lies in its flexibility and limitless possibility. You can create amazing pieces of art with few resources and minimal mess. Plus, mistakes are much easier to fix digitally! It does not mean though that traditional art is any less invaluable, as it lays the foundation of understanding art at its core.

Branching Into Digital Art

So now that you know what digital art is, where should you start? The first thing to do is to familiarize yourself with the tools. Understand how your drawing tablet and stylus work and experiment with different settings on your digital art software.

So, are you ready to start your digital art adventure? Good! Remember that the journey is your canvas, and the digital tools are your brushes. There is no right or wrong in art, only personification of thoughts. Don't worry about defining your artwork; let it define you instead. Just hold on tight to your stylus, and on this exciting digital ride, let your creativity run wild!

basics of graphic design and digital illustration

Gear up to dive into the sparkling sea of creativity; today, we're exploring the exciting world of graphic design and digital illustration. It's a true blend of technology and art. Picture painting but with a computer and software instead of traditional brushes and canvases. Exciting, isn't it?

To begin with, graphic design is a type of visual communication where we use images, symbols, colors, and text to convey messages. It's all around us, from the packaging on our cereal boxes to the advertisements on billboards. Digital illustration, on the other hand, is creating art using digital tools.

It's like drawing on a tablet connected to a computer, which brings your masterpiece to life on-screen!

Now, let's unpack some of the essential elements in graphic design and digital illustration. Just like every budding artist needs a sketchbook or paintbrush, a graphic designer's essential tool is a device, most likely a computer, with a design software installed. You might have heard some of their names: Adobe Photoshop, Illustrator, or Procreate. These are the virtual playgrounds where the magic of digital creation happens!

An exciting thing about digital art is using layers. Imagine having sheets of glass stacked on top of each other. Now, if you draw a sun on one layer (or 'sheet of glass') and a cloud on another, you can move them around separately. The sun can rise or set, the cloud can float around your canvas, and you can even make them disappear without affecting the other elements in your drawing. Isn't that great?

Color is another crucial factor in graphic design and digital illustration. Unlike your traditional paint palette, here we have an unlimited array of colors. It's like a giant rainbow just at your fingertips! Different colors can provoke different emotions and reactions, so picking the right one is incredibly important. A general rule is cool colors like blues and greens can give a calming effect, while warm colors like reds and yellows are energetic.

Shapes and lines, whether geometric or organic, are significant components in design. They help to define spaces, draw attention, or create a rhythm in your design. Think of shapes in design as building blocks, they can be used individually or combined to create something meticulously intricate.

Now, let's talk about something called 'typography'. It's fancy talk for the art of arranging letters and text. Just like in your favorite comic books or animated movies, the way text looks and feels can tell a story on its own. Maybe the words are painted on a banner flapping in the wind or carved out of a magical tree. Your imagination is really the limit!

Typography also involves choosing the right font, which is really just a design for a set of letters. Though it may sound simple, this step can sometimes make or break your design. The correct font can help your message stand clear, while a mismatched one might confuse an audience.

Another cool thing about digital art is the concept of scalability, which means your artwork can be resized without losing its quality. Picture this, you worked hard making a beautiful butterfly on your computer. Now, you can make it as small as a ladybug or as big as a kite and it will still look just as wonderful!

Producing successful graphic design and digital illustrations means considering all these elements like a culinary recipe, mixing ingredients in the right proportion and sequence. You might want to create a whole scene with different characters using shapes, or make a classic poster with cool typography. You could even combine everything and create a fantasy world all on your own!

Becoming a graphic designer or a digital illustrator is fun, thrilling, and requires a lot of practice. It might seem overwhelming initially, but remember, even the most seasoned designers once started where you are right now. Every masterpiece starts with a single line or a single idea. So, have patience, keep practicing and continue experimenting.

online resources and communities for young artists

Imagine having your very own toolbox—a box carrying the magic paintbrushes of Picasso or the sharp sketch pencils of Leonardo. But this toolbox isn't physical, it's virtual; it's not from a nearby art shop, but it's just a click away. Even better—it's not just filled with tools, but also teachers and friends who love art just like you. Useful, isn't it? That's what we're going to explore!

First off, let's delve into resources. Online resources are like your secret guides—they are places on the internet that allow you to learn, practice and improve your skills. Websites like 'Art For Kids Hub' and 'Hello Kids' become your virtual classrooms with hundreds of free activities, drawing tutorials, and coloring pages. On YouTube channels like 'Fun2draw,' an artist guides you on how to draw fun and cute characters, while the 'Cartooning Club' teaches how to draw your favorite comic characters.

Got a tablet or smartphone? Great! Apps like 'Tayasui Sketches,' 'Adobe Photoshop Sketch,' and 'Paper by WeTransfer' offer amazing drawing tools and brushes for you to create digital art. You can also play around with colors, shapes, and even animate your drawings using 'FlipaClip.' All you need to do is download these apps and start doodling!

Now, on to art communities. These are online spaces where you can connect with other young artists around the world. 'DeviantArt,' the world's largest online art community, is a fantastic place to explore. It has a special section called 'Young Artists' Club' which allows you to delve deep into the mesmerizing world of art. But remember, always seek help from an adult to set up your profile and check privacy settings to stay safe online.

Ever thought about sharing your artwork with millions of people around the world? There's an app for that. 'PopJam' is a safe and fun platform where you can post your art, take part in challenges, and get feedback from other kids. You can follow your favorite artists, learn from them, and become a part of the creative process.

For those who are interested in comics and cartoons, websites like 'Pixton' and 'MakeBeliefs-Comix' let you create your own comic strips. You can experiment with characters, write dialogues, and even print your finished masterpieces.

Starting to feel like digital art is your call? 'Tynker' is a coding platform that allows you to design and animate. It combines the thrill of video game design with art, turning your stories into interactive animations. It's like becoming an artist and a game designer at the same time!

Whether you are in rural Arkansas or bustling New York City, these resources can reach you. From the free drawing lessons on 'Art For Kids Hub' to sharing your artwork on 'PopJam,' these resources provide you with a vast array of online platforms to learn, create, and share. The sky is the limit for your imagination and creativity.

The world outside is full of splendid colors, shapes, and stories waiting to be captured by you. So, go on, explore these exciting online resources and communities, and most importantly—keep creating and sharing your beautiful art. Remember, every artist starts somewhere, and these resources might be your first step into the fabulous world of art and illustration. Happy creating!

9 /
sharing your art

tips for presenting and sharing art in galleries and online

YOU'VE MASTERED THE TECHNIQUES, and now have a collection of splendid artworks just waiting to be shown to the world. This chapter is going to take you on a fun journey into the exciting world of art presentation. Whether you want to exhibit your art in a fancy gallery or share it with thousands of people on the internet, we will go through tips that can help you make it happen!

First things first, you need to remember that your art is your story. So, when you're preparing to display your work, think about how you can showcase your artistic journey and individuality. You see, whether it's a local art gallery or an online platform, you're not just sharing a piece of artwork; you're sharing an extension of yourself.

Let's talk about galleries first. These places are like the stages of a theater, where your art gets to be the star. Just like in a play, the set-up matters. Think about the best way to display your artwork. Should it be in a sequence? Could different pieces be grouped together? Could a particularly powerful piece stand alone? The goal is to create a flow that guides the viewer through your collection.

Now, one more thing about galleries - they often have guidelines and restrictions about what and how you can display. Don't panic! This is not as scary as it sounds. It could be as simple as ensuring your artwork can hang properly on their walls or that it fits within a certain space. Make sure to have a chat with the gallery owner about what's acceptable and plan accordingly.

Let's shift gears slightly and talk about sharing art online. In the digital world, practically anyone can quickly become an artist with global exposure. It feels fantastic to have people from different corners of the world appreciating your work, doesn't it? But how can you harness the power of the internet to showcase your beautiful creations? Here's how.

First, you need to have high-quality

photographs of your art. This means clear, well-lit images that truly show off the detail and effort you've put into your work. If you're not sure how to take good pictures, ask a friendly adult or older sibling for help.

Now, once you have your photos, it's time to pick the right online platform. There are several options like personal websites, blogs, social media sites, and online art galleries. Choose a platform that suits your style and your audience. For instance, if your artwork has a lot of youthful energy, vibrant colors and quirky shapes, Instagram is a great platform. It's popular with younger audiences who'd probably love your style!

Once you've chosen your online space, be consistent and regular in your posts. You can even share snippets of your art process or shots of your art supplies. People are often curious about the "behind-the-scenes" making of the artwork.

Feedback is another vital part of presenting and sharing your art, both in galleries and online. It's like a guide showing you where to go next. Be open to it. Not all feedback will be a shower of compliments and that's okay. Constructive criticism can help you grow more than you think. Take it with grace, learn from it, and keep on improving.

Making your mark in the world of art might

seem like a huge mountain to climb, but remember, even the longest journey starts with one small step. Present your artwork to the world with pride and confidence, whether you choose the traditional gallery route or the exciting digital platform.

Artists, picking up a brush or sketch pen and creating beautiful artwork is a unique and thrilling journey. But it's equally important to learn how to share that beauty with the world. You now possess the knowledge to display your work skillfully and effectively. Your vibrant strokes of brilliance deserve to reach more and more people, and these tips can help you do just that. So go ahead, prepare your stage (or screen), and get ready to let your art dazzle the world! Don't hide your light; let it shine for everyone to see!

building an art portfolio

After learning all about the fun tools and techniques, I bet you're wondering what to do next, right? Well, it's time to get serious about preparing your art portfolio. Now, don't let the word 'serious' scare you, because building an art portfolio is just a fancy way of saying "Hey, here's a collection of my super cool artwork!"

The first and perhaps the most exciting step in

building an art portfolio is to create some art. Pretty obvious, right? But those fresh sheets of paper aren't going to draw on themselves. You can choose to sketch your favorite pet, paint a pretty landscape, or go totally out-of-the-box with abstract art or surrealism. Let your imagination run free and wild. Whatever you do, remember one keyword-variety. Include still life, portraits, landscape, and maybe even a comic strip or a digitally created piece. The more variety, the more you can showcase your versatility, and guess what? People love an artist who can do it all.

Next, we need to consider quality. Now, you might be thinking, "But I'm just learning, how can I make sure my work is high quality?" Well, when we talk about quality, we don't mean you need to paint like Vincent Van Gogh right away. Quality means doing the best you can do right now. Each piece you create should be something you're proud to hang on your wall, or share with your friends and family. It doesn't matter if it took you an hour or a week to complete, as long as you've put in your best effort and learned something new, it belongs in your portfolio.

So, you have your drawings and paintings ready, but that's just one part of the process. An art portfolio needs to be more than a pile of papers.

You need to arrange your artworks in a way that tells a story – your art journey. Start with the pieces you're most proud of, then go chronologically, showing progress over time, and finish with your recent artworks. This way, anyone going through your portfolio will get a sense of your artistic journey and growth.

Now comes a fun part, picking a portfolio. Remember, this isn't just a place to store your works; it represents you as an artist. Imagine if someone gave you a beautifully decorated gift box. Wouldn't that make you excited to see what's inside? Consider your portfolio the same way. You want to make people excited to see your artwork before they've even opened it. A simple binder with clear sheet protectors can work, or you can be more creative with an art folder or portfolio case you've decorated yourself.

Lastly, never underestimate the power of a neat, well-organized presentation. Arranging your works neatly isn't just about looking professional, it's about showing that you care about your creations. After all your hard work, do your pieces justice by presenting them in an appealing way that best showcases them.

Building an art portfolio is not a one-time activity; it's like a journey that goes hand in hand with your art adventures. As you explore new techniques, see new places, or get inspired by new experiences, your portfolio should continue to grow and evolve. It's your art diary, a reflection of your journey so far, and a taste of where you're going.

Remember, the goal of an art portfolio isn't to make you anxious or stressed. Instead, it's there to celebrate your creativity. Realistically, not every piece you create will end up in a museum, and that's okay! Art is about expression, learning, growing, and most importantly, having fun. Every brush stroke, pencil line, or digital art pixel you lay down is a step forward on your artistic journey.

navigating feedback and criticism

In the world of art, feedback and criticism are as certain as brush strokes on a canvas. You see, being artists, we put a piece of ourselves out into the world every time we share our work. That very act takes courage, my friends. And the responses you get? They'll shape you, teach you, make you stronger, and help you to grow. Let's begin by understanding them better.

Feedback and criticism generally come in two forms: constructive and destructive. Constructive feedback is designed to build you up. It's helpfully honest, pointing out areas where you can improve while also acknowledging the things you've done well. Constructive criticism is a gift, wrapped in honesty and often tied with a bow of experience. It helps you become a better artist because it shows you how to improve and learn, without tearing down your confidence.

On the other hand, destructive criticism is not so helpful. It may feel like it tears you down, focusing on the negative without offering any useful insights. It could be harsh and dismissive. However, it's essential to understand that this type of criticism reflects more about the person giving it than it says about your work.

Now, understanding feedback and criticism is one thing - dealing with it is another. To start, look at feedback as knowledge – knowledge you can use to refine your work and develop your unique style further. You will never agree with all the feedback you receive, and you don't have to. The art world is beautifully subjective - what works wonders for one person may not resonate with another. The key is figuring out what advice resonates with you and aligns with your vision as an artist.

Receiving comments about your work can sometimes sting, especially when you've poured your heart and soul into it. That's completely normal, and it's okay to feel upset. Give yourself permission to feel, but once that initial shock or upset fades, try to look at the critique objectively. Ask yourself, "Does this feedback help me grow as an artist? Can I use it to enhance my work and my skill?" If the answer's yes, then it's a golden chance to learn something new!

Remember, it's also okay to disagree with feedback but do it respectfully. You're the artist. You're the one in control of your art. No one else. So listen, thank them for their time, and then decide whether you want to incorporate their feedback or not.

Now, we've been talking about others' feedback, but it's equally important to learn to self-critique. This practice involves objectively reviewing your work and identifying areas that worked out well and those that could use improvement. Look at each piece you create, analyze it, learn from it, and then carry those lessons forward to your next artwork.

When it comes to destructive criticism, that's a slightly different beast to tackle. It can be harsh and sometimes even plain mean. Receiving such critique can hurt, especially from the people you look up to or admire. The key is to remember that this sort of criticism often tells more about the critic than about your art. Maybe they're having a terrible day. Or perhaps they just can't appreciate the style you're working in, but that doesn't mean your work is bad.

In situations like these, remember the old saying, "You can be the ripest, juiciest peach in the world, and there's still going to be someone who hates peaches." That's life! And it's especially true for artists - you won't be able to please everyone. And guess what? That's perfectly okay.

To navigate this tricky path, maintain a strong belief in yourself and your capabilities. Your worth as an artist is not defined by someone's heated comment; it's defined by your passion, dedication, and the joy you find in art. Allow yourself to extract any useful tidbits from the rubble, then move on and continue creating.

As we wrap up this chapter, remember that feedback and criticism are all part of the journey. They're signs that you're growing, learning, and, most importantly, creating. So take heart in the fact that every comment, every critique, and every piece of feedback you receive is actually a stepping stone to becoming a better artist.

10 / interactive art projects

step-by-step art projects for various skill levels

LET'S ease into the exciting realm of art and start with a simple project great for beginners. You'll need paper, a pencil, an eraser and lots of enthusiasm. Geometric shapes are fundamental to all art. Therefore, our starter project involves drawing a basic geometric shape, such as a square or a triangle. Here's how you do it.

1. Take a deep breath. All great art is born from calmness.
   2. Place the pencil lightly against your paper.

3. Now, try a triangle first. Start from one point and draw a slanting line down.

4. Next, draw a straight horizontal line from the end of this line.

5. Finally, connect the open point from the horizontal line back to the starting point.

6. Voila! Your first geometric shape!

Now that we have warmed up, let's try a more intermediate project. How about an animal sketch? Let's try a cat, combining geometric shapes and simple lines.

1. Just like before, gather all your tools, clear your mind, and take your position.

2. A circle is the perfect start for the cat's head. Draw it clean and smooth.

3. For the body, add an oval shape just below the head.

4. The ears of the cat are nothing but triangles. Draw two on top of the circle.

5. The eyes can be two smaller circles inside the bigger circle.

6. Draw some curved lines for whiskers, a

triangle for the nose, and an inverted "Y" for the mouth.

7. Complete the body with lines for legs and a wavy line for the tail.

8. Don't forget to put small circles at the ends of the legs for paws!

Getting the hang of it now? Fantastic! Finally, in our conquest of the art world, let's tackle a slightly complex project for advanced learners - a landscape painting. You'll need paints, brushes, some water, and a canvas or thick paper. Remember, the purpose isn't to create a masterpiece, but to challenge yourself and enjoy the process.

1. A landscape starts from the sky. Mix blue and white, and create long strokes across the top half of your canvas.

2. For the mountains, mix shades of gray and green. Paint them just below your sky.

3. The grasslands are next. Create them by brushing shades of green and brown.

4. Place a circle for the sun in your sky, painting inside with bold yellow and soft oranges.

5. Use back and forth strokes to create the illusion of a path in between the grasslands.

6. Finally, add details like trees, flowers, or a small hut using dark and light tones.

There you have it! You have now taken your first steps into the vast and enriching universe of art, tried a hand at various projects. I hope you have realized two important things - that creating art is about much more than just the finished product, and that each one of your strokes carries a vitality of its own that reflects your unique perspective.

group projects and collaborative ideas

Can you recall a time when you and a friend decorated your tree-house or pieced together a puzzle? Did you both have similar ideas? More often than not, you must have found that two brains brought together resulted in better colors on the walls, or the puzzle was completed faster. Collaboration can boost both the quality and the speed of creation, just like it did in your tree-house or with that tricky puzzle.

. . .

Let's step inside an imaginary art club. Here, young artists like yourselves gather each week to create something stunning, just for the sheer joy of it. Some might be good at sketching, others at choosing eye-catching color combinations, and a few might have a knack for creating three-dimensional models. Now here's a thing. When everyone brings their unique skills to the table, what happens? Voila! A beautiful collage of creativity comes to life.

Here's why this works so magically. As we've discussed throughout this book, every artist has their strengths and areas of expertise, which means, stunning as it may sound, there's no artist out there who's fabulous at everything. In a group project, you, as an artist, can shine by bringing your strengths into play while learning from the expertise of others. For instance, if you lack experience using pastels, but your fellow artist excels at it, what better chance to learn and improve?

Plus, group work can also serve as a way to push outside the comfort zones of individual ideas and styles. Want to try some graffiti but are unsure how to go about it? Recruit a fellow budding artist who knows the ropes. A group setting creates a safety net and allows you to experiment with new approaches and techniques fearlessly.

Now, remember those famous cartoon characters, 'The Penguins of Madagascar,' who always said, "Just smile and wave, boys, smile and wave." Well, in the world of art, it's "Just share and learn, artists, share and learn!" In our art club, you might discover that your understanding of proportions dazzles others, and someone else's techniques with watercolors make you exclaim, "How on earth did you do that?" That's the beauty of groups. They provide a platform for you to share your strengths and learn from others.

A great example of collaborative art from history is the intricate ceiling of the Sistine Chapel, painted by Michelangelo and his apprentices. When you think about it, even a renowned artist like Michelangelo needed the help of others to complete his stunning masterpiece.

. . .

However, collaboration isn't all rainbows and butterflies. There can be conflicts when several artists work together. Some may want to paint the sky pink, while others may insist on blue. But here's the secret - these conflicts often result in the most creative solutions. Just think Cinderella's mice friends and the debates they must have had while making her dress!

When you face a disagreement in a group project, stay calm, listen to the other person, and express your ideas respectfully. The aim is not to win the argument but to find a solution that makes your group's artwork better. In fact, resolving disagreements can lead to friendships that last beyond the course of the project.

In the world of professional art and illustration, teamwork is also enormous. You might be hired to work as part of a team to illustrate a children's book or create themed murals for a hotel. Learning to collaborate now will prepare you for your future career, boosting your ability to create dazzling illustrations that can move and inspire people.

Sarah Michaels

diy art crafts and activities

You've learned so much about the art world, about illustration, styles, materials, and now it's time to plunge into some fantastic arts and crafts. These activities will spark your creativity and might even prepare you for pursuing your future career in arts and illustration! This dynamic chapter will be filled with mesmerizing art activities that you can make right at home.

First, let's set things up for our creative adventure. Ensure you have the essential art supplies like pencils, paints, brushes, scissors, glue, and don't forget, paper! Got everything? Perfect! Make sure to wear an old shirt, or an apron to protect your clothes, as some activities can get a tad bit messy, but hey, that's the fun part, right?

We'll start with an easy one - paper mosaics. Mosaics are magnificent art pieces made by fitting together smaller pieces, like a jigsaw puzzle. Traditional mosaics often use tiles or stones, but we'll use colored paper instead. Draw out a simple design on a piece of cardboard. It could be anything - from a beautiful butterfly to your favorite cartoon character. Then begin filling the design with small squares of colored paper, using glue to stick them down. Don't forget to overlap the pieces slightly to ensure none of the cardboard is visible. Keep going, and voila! Your striking paper mosaic is complete!

Next up, we have abstract bubble painting. Sounds intriguing, right? Wait till you try it! All you need are food coloring, dish soap, straws, and water. Mix the soap, coloring, and water in different containers then blow into it with a straw, creating oodles of colorful bubbles. Then, quickly lay a piece of paper over the bubbles, and you'll have a captivating bubble print! It's a beautiful, spontaneous art form, just like abstract art itself!

Our third DIY art craft is string art. This takes a little more patience and precision, but believe me, it's worth it. You will need a wooden board, nails, a hammer, and of course, string or colored yarn. Draw a basic design on the board, something like a heart or a star, then hammer in nails along the design line. Once you are done, tie the string or yarn at a starting nail and start winding it around the other nails. Keep switching back and forth until your design is filled, and you've got yourself a super cool string art display!

Guess what? We're going to be archaeologists now! Well, sort of. We're making our cave drawings. With white, brown and black crayons (or charcoal if you have it), draw on a piece of sandpaper to mimic cave walls. Instead of usual illustrations, create symbols and 'cave paintings' inspired by ancient art. You'll be surprised at how expressive these stick-and-dot figures can be. Oh, and don't forget to 'sign' your artwork with a handprint, just like our ancestors did.

Finally, let's take a trip to Italy and create our Venetian masks. These can be simple or elaborate, depending on your patience and skill. Start with a basic mask template (you can find these online), then cut out and decorate with paint, glitter, feathers, beads, whatever you like! Let your creativity go wild!

· · ·

Taking part in DIY art activities, like these, helps us explore and grow as budding artists. It allows us to venture into various types of art forms while pushing us to use our imagination, creativity and problem-solving skills. Plus, they are super fun to do!

Keep in mind, art is all about expressing yourself. Your masterpieces reflect your personality, your thoughts, your ideas, and your dreams. So, don't worry about getting everything 'perfect.' Art is never about perfection; it's about expression and creation. So keep creating and keep expressing. Your passion and hard work are the key ingredients to the amazing artist cocktail!

Keep on experimenting, keep on crafting, and before you know it, you'll be crafting your art career out of the skills you've built. So, let's get those hands dirty and craft some beautiful memories!

conclusion

Art has a way of speaking to us, telling stories, and teaching lessons without saying a word. From a single stroke of a paintbrush to an elaborate mural on a city wall, art is a language the whole world speaks. When you pick up a pencil, a brush, or shape clay, you're not just creating a picture or sculpture. You're telling your own story. Just imagine, what could be more exciting than that?

Art allows you to explore a world full of imagination, expression, and discovery. So, whether you're sketching stick figures or painting beautiful landscapes, remember, there's no right or wrong in art. There's just the joy of creation.

However, making art isn't always about how well you handle a brush or how accurately you can draw a portrait. In fact, the great thing about art is

Conclusion

that it is subjective. In other words, everyone has a unique interpretation when they look at a piece of art, just as every artist has a unique way of expressing their ideas and feelings. Therefore, it's perfectly okay if your art doesn't look like someone else's. Your artwork is yours, and the uniqueness is what makes it special.

Think about your favorite picture book. What makes it so special? Maybe it's the thrilling adventure, the funny characters, or the heartfelt message. But have you ever thought about the illustrations? Those colorful scenes that make the story come alive are created by talented artists and illustrators. They've used their creative skills to craft a visual world, all from their imagination. And guess what? You can do that too!

Now, let's talk about how to nurture this creative spark within you. Like any other skill, artistic talent flourishes with practice. So, draw, sketch, paint, sculpt... every day if you can. Try out different styles, techniques, and mediums. You might discover you love watercolors more than oils, or you might find that the simplicity of pencil drawings is more your style. And don't forget to explore the digital world of art. Creating artwork on a tablet or a computer can be just as fulfilling as traditional methods.

Conclusion

Remember, it's okay to make mistakes in art. In fact, they often lead to great discoveries. Maybe you spilled some paint on your sketchbook, but instead of seeing it as a blob, you find a shape within it, a new idea forms and it sets you off on a new creative venture.

What if you want to turn this passion for art into a career? Then, hurray! There are countless opportunities available in the art world. You could be an illustrator, creating vibrant images for books. Or perhaps a concept artist, designing extraordinary creatures and worlds for video games and movies. Maybe even a teacher, inspiring future generations of artists. The sky's the limit!

To pursue art as a career, learning and honing your skills is essential. Plenty of artists attend art schools to get formal training, while others are largely self-taught. Whatever path you choose, remember that critical to your artistic journey is the willingness to learn, adapt, and grow.

But before you go forward, it's important to remember - pursuit of art, like any other career, requires dedication and patience. There might be days when you feel like the muse has left you and your sketchbook is full of half-finished ideas. But remember, creativity is not a tap that you can turn on and off. It comes in waves and sometimes calm seas. Be patient, keep trying new things, and most importantly have fun with your art.

Art offers a way to express yourself that words might fail to capture, a tool to create your own unique version of reality, and a medium to share your inner world. An artist is a storyteller, a visionary; their canvas, clay, or computer screen are just the tools to share these stories and visions.

And you, young explorers of the world of art, are among those future visionaries. The possibility that you could someday add your colors, ideas, and vision to this wonderful world of art is tremendously exciting. It's a journey that is bound to be filled with learning, exploration, and plenty of joy. Labored over a drawing for hours only to be disappointed with the result? No worries! Every stroke, every shade added value to your growth as an artist. Resulting in a triumph in itself.

steps to continue growing as an artist

While you've already taken the thrilling leap into the world of art and illustration, in this chapter, we will talk about fascinating steps you can continue to take to keep growing as an artist.

Step 1: Embrace the Art of Learning

Conclusion

The fantastic thing about art, or any creative field for that matter, is that you can never hit the 'pause' button on learning. There's always something new to discover, understand, or experiment with. So, keep an open mind and a brave heart. Attend workshops; they are magical pits stops on your artistic journey where you can replenish your creativity. Make friends with books – like this cool one you're reading about a career in art and illustration, eh? Experiment with different mediums – oils, charcoal, digital, or even mixed media. The world of art is your oyster!

Step 2: Embrace a Sketchpad

A sketchpad is a great friend that's always there for you, ready for your doodling adventures. Whether it's a quick scribble while waiting for the school bus or a detailed drawing on a lazy afternoon, your sketchpad is your safe space. Drawing daily can help strengthen your skills and infused your artistic sense with more confidence.

Step 3: Find Your Artistic Voice

Just like fingers' prints, every artist has a unique style. It's what sets you apart and leaves an imprint on your art. So, explore different genres and mediums until you find what you're most passionate about. Is it story-driven comic sketches or landscape paintings? Cartoony illustrations or complex abstract collages? Give yourself room to explore and find your artistic voice.

Step 4: Get Inspired by the Greats

Every great artist was once a beginner who looked up to the legendary masters. Picasso, Van Gogh, Da Vinci – these were artists who transformed the canvas of their time and continue to inspire millions. So, spend some time absorbing their work, their techniques, their stories. While you're on this learning voyage, remember to not merely imitate but incorporate what you learn into your unique style.

Step 5: Find a Tribe

Wait a moment, a tribe? Yes, indeed! By a tribe, we mean a group of like-minded artistic buddies who inspire and encourage each other. Join local art clubs, attend community art events, or even find a virtual group online. The key is to support and receive support. Art, like any journey, is more enjoyable when traveled with companions.

Step 6: Celebrate Progress, Not Just Perfection

There will be times when your artwork won't turn out as you had imagined. Those smudged lines, unbalanced compositions, or "not quite right" colors can leave you feeling a bit disheartened. But remember, every mishap, every 'oops' moment is a step towards betterment. Celebrate your growth, not just the perfect outcomes. They're all part of your vivid artistic journey.

These steps might seem like many, but that is the enchanting part about art – it's a journey with so many avenues to explore. When you look back after a few years, you will realize that every little effort, each experimental stroke, every moment spent appreciating a masterpiece, and even the seemingly "failed" projects contributed to your growth as an artist.

And perhaps the most wonderful part about this journey is that as an artist, you never truly 'arrive.' There's always a new horizon to set sail for, a fresh technique to master, or a challenging theme to tackle. So, continue to evolve, and let your art grow as you do. Your art comes from a place deep within your heart - a place that keeps expanding as you collect experiences in life.

final thoughts

Being an artist isn't just about creating beautiful pieces of art, it's also about the passion that kindles deep within you. Remember when we talked about some of the world's most celebrated artists, like Michelangelo and Van Gogh? Each one of them had a fierce love for art which

Conclusion

refused to be dimmed, despite the challenges they faced.

Let me tell you a secret. The most vibrant paintings, the most enchanting sculptures, the most captivating sketches - they all flow from an artist's hearth of passion. If you love what you do, it will reflect in your work. Keep that passion ablaze, young artists! Fuel it with your dedication, your astute observations, and your relentless imagination.

Now, let's address something quite important - mistakes. We've all heard of that pesky little word, haven't we? In your journey as an artist, you are bound to make a few... probably even a hundred more. You might sketch a line too long, paint a shade too dark, or even smudge a nearly perfect artwork. But guess what? That's perfectly okay! In fact, it's more than okay; it's fantastic!

Why, you might ask? Because every mistake you make, every sketch you redo, every canvas you repaint, each one is a step forward on your path as an artist. Mistakes are opportunities to learn and grow. They teach you what not to do next time, and that is just as important as knowing what to do.

Here's another crucial point, my young creators: comparison. When you're starting out and still polishing your craft, it's easy to look at those around you—who may be more advanced—and feel discouraged. Don't! Everyone's path is as unique as their art style. Some might sprint towards their goals, while others take a gentle stroll. Both ways are completely alright! Your journey is your own, set your own pace. A masterpiece after all, takes time doesn't it?

More than anything else, be patient and be kind—to your own self. Skills take time to hone, talents take time to sparkle. You'll find yourself every day a little better than the previous one if you keep going. Discouragement could sneak in through the door, but remember, it's your house, and you can always show discouragement the way back out.

One ultimate treasure that artists possess is their imagination. It is your magic carpet that can take you to the most surprising of places and the most colourful of worlds. Cherish that imagination of yours. Feed it with a variety of experiences, observations, and emotions. With a colorful imagination, you will never run out of new ideas to put onto your canvas.

And finally, remember, art is an expression of you! Your happiness, your sadness, your excitement, your fears—they are unique to you. Every artwork you create is a reflection of your thoughts, your dreams, your perception of the world. Don't

Conclusion

be afraid to express yourself, to share a piece of you with the world. Because the world, my young friend, is waiting to see the wonders you can create.

Well, it's time for this chapter to end, but remember, your artistic journey has only just embarked! Keep your brush ready, your sketch pad handy, always be open to inspiration, and let your imagination run wild. With verve in your heart and a twinkle in your eye, step forward into the wonderful world of art that awaits just for you.

Cheers to the enchanting adventure ahead of you, future world-renowned artists! You've got this!

appendex

resources for further learning

While our journey together in this book was a taste of all the fantastic stuff you can do with art, there is so much more waiting to be discovered. All it takes is a bit of curiosity and a thirst for creativity.

Still eager for more? Fantastic, let's get started!

First on our list, let's talk about books. You might think, "But hey, aren't we just done reading one?" And you're absolutely correct! But remember, with art, there's always more to learn.

1. "Ed Emberley's Drawing Book: Make a World" is one of the best art books out there for kids your age. Ed Emberley inspires children to draw using simple shapes. Even if you can draw a

square, triangle, or circle - you'd be amazed at the world you can create!

2. "Art for Kids: Drawing" by Kathryn Temple is another fantastic book. It breaks down the basics of drawing into easy-to-understand terms. You don't need to know big, fancy art words to be an artist; sometimes all you need are your eyes and your imagination.

Moving on to the digital world, there are some fascinating websites and online platforms where you can learn more about art and illustration and even share your artwork.

1. Art for Kids Hub is a fantastic online resource packed with drawing lessons ideal for young artists like you. The Hub family will guide you step by step to create your next masterpiece.

2. Artsonia Kids Art Museum is another cool site. This virtual museum is filled to the brim with art masterpieces made by kids from all over the world. You can even submit your artwork and see it on display for the whole world to admire!

3. Want a site that combines learning with games? Then you should check out Tate Kids. With art quizzes, guides, and even awesome art history games, learning art has never been more fun!

What about YouTube, you say? Of course, we

can't forget that! There are countless YouTube channels dedicated to teaching art.

1. "Art for Kids Hub" has a YouTube channel filled with hundreds of fun art lessons. Best of all, you can pause, rewind, and rewatch as much as you want until you are happy with your drawing.

2. "Happy Drawings - Draw Cute and Easy Things" is a channel that might pique your interest. The channel helps you create adorable drawings—sometimes with a fun twist!

Finally, for the tech-savvy artist, we have some amazing drawing apps that can help you learn and practice.

1. "Procreate" is a fantastic app for iPad users. It has a range of brushes and tools for you to play around with and create digital art.

2. "Sketches School" is another brilliant app for creating digital art, with a clean and easy-to-use interface suitable for your age.

The beauty of art and illustration is that it's a never-ending journey of learning and creativity. The more you explore, the more you grow as an artist. And remember, it's not only about becoming a professional artist one day; it's about enjoying the process, making mistakes, and having fun along the way. These resources will be your companions in this journey, guiding you and inspiring you.

Appendex

So keep discovering, keep practicing, and keep creating! Art is everywhere around you—you just need the eyes to see it and the heart to appreciate and create it.

Milton Keynes UK
Ingram Content Group UK Ltd.
UKHW021647201124
451457UK00008B/166